# This book belongs to.....

_______________________________

_______________________________

Mirror, mirror, in the car.
Who is hiding in the back?

Little spider with eight legs,
Dreaming **BIG** of worldly webs.

Looking through the mirror glass,

Watching landscapes flashing past.

When the web is broken up,
Weaving back is no big ask.

When the wind begins to puff,

Pants go flying –

That's enough!

Time for lunch!
But who is that?!

Fly!
Grasshopper!!
Ladybug!!!

What luck!
I think I'm
winning!

We are snack!
... But wait a minute!?

Table seats are FOUR not one!
Spider's plan is to have FUN!
Vegetarian Meals for Arachnid

Let's see...
DEEP BLUE SEA !
Let's see...
MOUNTAINS HIGH !

Let's see...
FOREST GREEN !
Let's see...
CITY LIGHTS !

Mirror, mirror, in the car.
Who is hiding in the back?

Little spider with his friends,
Planning travels...

On the  PLANE !?

# Fun Facts about Spiders

Spider's silk is stronger than steel
and all spiders can spin silk

Spiders can walk on walls and ceilings,
and some can even jump!

Spiders can have up to 8 eyes!

There is a "vegeterian" spider called Bagheera
Kiplingi, found in Central America

Not all spiders make webs and some live
under water

Spiders blood is blue!

There are Giant Spiders, Daddy Long
Legs Spiders, Wolf Spiders, Garden
Spiders, Crab Spiders, Money Spiders....

Reggie... is a Unique Spider!

For my sons, Jack and James.

## Author's note:

This story was born from a curious little mystery: no matter how often I cleaned the cobwebs from my car's rear view mirror, they always reappeared overnight - delicate, determined and freshly spun. One day, while driving, I finally spotted the tiny culprit clinging to his shimmering thread, swaying gently in the breeze. That moment sparked the idea for Reggie - a tiny spider with dreams as vast as the world and friends that see beyond first impressions.

Adventure often begins in the most unexpected places and even the smallest of creatures carry big stories.

Published by The Ink Tales
Watford, Herfordshire, UK
Author © Ewa Kowalska 2026. Illustrator © Olga Sall 2026.
Editor: Ewa Kowalska



ISBN 9781919421933 (paperback)      ISBN 9781919421957 (oprawa miękka)
ISBN 9781919421919 (hardcover)      ISBN 9781919421926 (oprawa twarda)
ISBN 9781919421902 (ebook)          ISBN 9781919421940 (oprawa elektroniczna)